PENGUIN BOOKS — GREAT IDEAS

Man Alone with Himself

Friedrich Nietzsche

1844–1900

Friedrich Nietzsche

Man Alone with Himself

TRANSLATED BY MARION FABER,
STEPHEN LEHMANN AND R. J. HOLLINGDALE

PENGUIN BOOKS — GREAT IDEAS

PENGUIN BOOKS

Published by the Penguin Group
Penguin Books Ltd, 80 Strand, London WC2R ORL, England
Penguin Group (USA) Inc., 375 Hudson Street, New York, New York 10014, USA
Penguin Group (Canada), 90 Eglinton Avenue East, Suite 700, Toronto, Ontario, Canada M4P 2Y3
(a division of Pearson Penguin Canada Inc.)
Penguin Ireland, 25 St Stephen's Green, Dublin 2, Ireland
(a division of Penguin Books Ltd)
Penguin Group (Australia), 250 Camberwell Road, Camberwell, Victoria 3124, Australia
(a division of Pearson Australia Group Pty Ltd)
Penguin Books India Pvt Ltd, 11 Community Centre, Panchsheel Park, New Delhi – 110 017, India
Penguin Group (NZ), 67 Apollo Drive, Rosedale, North Shore 0632, New Zealand
(a division of Pearson New Zealand Ltd)
Penguin Books (South Africa) (Pty) Ltd, 24 Sturdee Avenue, Rosebank, Johannesburg 2196, South Africa

Penguin Books Ltd, Registered Offices: 80 Strand, London WC2R ORL, England

www.penguin.com

'Man Alone with Himself' taken from *Human, All Too Human*, first published in 1878 and
first published as a Penguin Classic in this translation by Marion Faber and Stephen
Lehmann, 1984. Translation copyright © Marion Faber, 1984
'The Free Spirit' and 'From High Mountains: Epode' taken from *Beyond Good and Evil: Prelude
to a Philosophy of the Future*, first published in 1886 and first published as a Penguin Classic in this
translation by R. J. Hollingdale, 1973. Translation copyright © R. J. Hollingdale, 1973, 1990
This selection first published 2008

015

All rights reserved

978-0-141-03668-7

www.greenpenguin.co.uk

Penguin Books is committed to a sustainable
future for our business, our readers and our planet.
This book is made from Forest Stewardship
Council™ certified paper.

Contents

The numbering system, starting at one, used for the individual sections is specific to this edition, as it was too cumbersome to begin the book with, for example, *Enemies of Truth* as number 483 as in the original work.

1   *Man Alone with Himself*

[handwritten: A belief in a Truth is more dangerous than can Un Truth]

1

Enemies of truth. Convictions are more dangerous enemies of truth than lies.

2

Topsy-turvy world. We criticize a thinker more sharply when he proposes a tenet that is disagreeable to us; and yet it would be more reasonable to do this when we find his tenet agreeable.

[handwritten: Attack our friends fiercely]

3

A person of character. It is much more common for a person to appear to have character because he always acts in accord with his temperament, rather than because he always acts in accord with his principles.

4

[handwritten: ot calm in the neurotic]

The one necessary thing. A person must have one or the other: either a disposition which is easygoing by nature, or else a disposition eased by art and knowledge.

5

Passion for things. He who directs his passion to things (the sciences, the national good, cultural interests, the arts) takes much of the fire out of his passion for people (even when they represent those things, as statesmen, philosophers, and artists represent their creations).

6

Calm in action. As a waterfall becomes slower and more floating as it plunges, so the great man of action will act with *greater* calm than could be expected from his violent desire before the deed.

7

Not too deep. People who comprehend a matter in all its depth seldom remain true to it forever. For they have brought its depths to the light; and then there is always much to see about it that is bad.

8

Idealists' delusion. All idealists imagine that the causes they serve are significantly better than the other causes in the world; they do not want to believe that if their cause is to flourish at all, it needs exactly the same foul-smelling manure that all other human undertakings require.

9

Self-observation. Man is very well defended against himself, against his own spying and sieges; usually he is able to make out no more of himself than his outer fortifications. The actual stronghold is inaccessible to him, even invisible, unless friends and enemies turn traitor and lead him there by a secret path.

10

The right profession. Men seldom endure a profession if they do not believe or persuade themselves that it is basically more important than all others. Women do the same with their lovers.

11

Nobility of mind. To a great degree, nobility of mind consists of good nature and lack of distrust, and thus contains precisely that which acquisitive and successful people so like to treat with superiority and scorn.

12

Destination and paths. Many people are obstinate about the path once it is taken, few people about the destination.

13

The infuriating thing about an individual way of living. People are always angry at anyone who chooses very individual standards for his life; because of the extraordinary treatment which that man grants to himself, they feel degraded, like ordinary beings.

14

Privilege of greatness. It is the privilege of greatness to grant supreme pleasure through trifling gifts.

15

Unwittingly noble. A man's behavior is unwittingly noble if he has grown accustomed never to want anything from men, and always to give to them.

16

Condition for being a hero. If a man wants to become a hero, the snake must first become a dragon: otherwise he is lacking his proper enemy.

17

Friend. Shared joy, not compassion, makes a friend.

18

Using high and low tides. For the purpose of knowledge, one must know how to use that inner current that draws us to a thing, and then the one that, after a time, draws us away from it.

19

Delight in oneself. 'Delight in an enterprise,' they say; but in truth it is delight in oneself, by means of an enterprise.

20

The modest one. He who is modest with people shows his arrogance all the more with things (the city, state, society, epoch, or mankind). That is his revenge.

21

Envy and jealousy. Envy and jealousy are the pudenda of the human soul. The comparison can perhaps be pursued further.

22

The most refined hypocrite. To speak about oneself not at all is a very refined form of hypocrisy.

23

Annoyance. Annoyance is a physical illness that is by no means ended simply by eliminating the cause of the annoyance.

24

Representatives of truth. The champions of truth are hardest to find, not when it is dangerous to tell it, but rather when it is boring.

25

More troublesome than enemies. When some reason (e.g., gratitude) obliges us to maintain the appearance of unqualified congeniality with people about whose own congenial behavior we are not entirely convinced, these people torment our imagination much more than do our enemies.

26

Out in nature. We like to be out in nature so much because it has no opinion about us.

27

Everyone superior in one thing. In civilized circumstances, everyone feels superior to everyone else in at least one way; this is the basis of the general goodwill, inasmuch as everyone is someone who, under certain conditions, can be of help, and need therefore feel no shame in allowing himself to be helped.

28

Reasons for consolation. When someone dies, we usually need reasons to be consoled, not so much to soften the force of our pain, as to excuse the fact that we feel consoled so easily.

29

Loyal to their convictions. The man who has a lot to do usually keeps his general views and opinions almost unchanged; as does each person who works in the service of an idea. He will never test the idea itself any more; he no longer has time for that. Indeed, it is contrary to his interest even to think it possible to discuss it.

30

Morality and quantity. One man's greater morality, in contrast to another's, often lies only in the fact that his goals are quantitatively larger. The other man is pulled down by occupying himself with small things, in a narrow sphere.

31

Life as the product of life. However far man may extend himself with his knowledge, however objective he may appear to himself – ultimately he reaps nothing but his own biography.

32

Iron necessity. Over the course of history, men learn that iron necessity is neither iron nor necessary.

33

From experience. That something is irrational is no argument against its existence, but rather a condition for it.

34

Truth. No one dies of fatal truths nowadays: there are too many antidotes.

35

Basic insight. There is no pre-established harmony between the furthering of truth and the good of mankind.

36

Human lot. Whoever thinks more deeply knows that he is always wrong, whatever his acts and judgments.

37

Truth as Circe. Error has turned animals into men; might truth be capable of turning man into an animal again?

38

Danger of our culture. We belong to a time in which culture is in danger of being destroyed by the means of culture.

39

Greatness means: to give a direction. No river is great and bounteous through itself alone, but rather because it takes up so many tributaries and carries them onwards: that makes it great. It is the same with all great minds. All that matters is that one man give the direction, which the many tributaries must then follow; it does not matter whether he is poorly or richly endowed in the beginning.

40

Weak conscience. Men who talk about their importance for mankind have a weak conscience about their common bourgeois honesty in keeping contracts or promises.

41

Wanting to be loved. The demand to be loved is the greatest kind of arrogance.

42

Contempt for people. The least ambiguous sign of a disdain for people is this: that one tolerates everyone else only as a means to *his* end, or not at all.

43

Disciples out of disagreement. Whoever has brought men to a state of rage against himself has always acquired a party in his favor, too.

44

Forgetting one's experiences. It is easy for a man who thinks a lot – and objectively – to forget his own experiences, but not the thoughts that were evoked by them.

45

Adhering to an opinion. One man adheres to an opinion because he prides himself on having come upon it by himself; another because he has learned it with effort, and is proud of having grasped it: thus both out of vanity.

46

Shunning the light. The good deed shuns the light as anxiously as the evil deed: the latter fears that, if it is known, pain (as punishment) will follow; the former fears that, if it is known, joy (that pure joy in oneself, which ceases as soon as it includes the satisfaction of one's vanity) will disappear.

47

The day's length. If a man has a great deal to put in them, a day will have a hundred pockets.

48

Tyrant-genius. If the soul stirs with an ungovernable desire to assert itself tyranically, and the fire is continually maintained, then even a slight talent (in politicians or artists) gradually becomes an almost irresistible force of nature.

49

The life of the enemy. Whoever lives for the sake of combating an enemy has an interest in the enemy's staying alive.

50

More important. The unexplained, obscure matter is taken as more important than the explained, clear one.

51

Evaluating services rendered. We evaluate services someone renders us according to the value that person places on them, not according to the value they have for us.

52

Unhappiness. The distinction that lies in being unhappy (as if to feel happy were a sign of shallowness, lack of ambition, ordinariness) is so great that when someone says, 'But how happy you must be!' we usually protest.

53

Fantasy of fear. The fantasy of fear is that malevolent, apelike goblin which jumps onto man's back just when he already has the most to bear.

54

Value of insipid opponents. Sometimes we remain true to a cause only because its opponents will not stop being insipid.

55

Value of a profession. A profession makes us thoughtless: therein lies its greatest blessing. For it is a bulwark, behind which we are allowed to withdraw when qualms and worries of a general kind attack us.

56

Talent. The talent of some men appears slighter than it is because they have always set themselves tasks that are too great.

57

Youth. The time of youth is disagreeable, for then it is not possible, or not reasonable, to be productive in any sense.

58

Goals too great. Who publicly sets himself great goals, and later realizes privately that he is too weak to accomplish them, does not usually have enough strength to revoke those goals publicly, either, and then inevitably becomes a hypocrite.

59

In the stream. Strong currents draw many stones and bushes along with them; strong minds many stupid and muddled heads.

60

Danger of intellectual liberation. When a man tries earnestly to liberate his intellect, his passions and desires secretly hope to benefit from it also.

61

Embodiment of the spirit. When a man thinks much and cleverly, not only his face, but also his body takes on a clever look.

62

Seeing poorly and hearing poorly. He who sees little, always sees less; he who hears poorly, always hears something more.

63

Self-enjoyment in vanity. The vain man wants not only to stand out, but also to feel outstanding, and therefore rejects no means to deceive and outwit himself. Not the opinion of others, but his opinion of their opinion is what he cares about.

64

Vain by way of an exception. When he is physically ill, the man who is usually self-sufficient is vain by way of an exception and responsive to fame and praise. In the proportion that he is losing himself, he must try to regain himself from the outside, using strangers' opinions.

65

The 'witty' ones. The man who seeks wit has no wit.

66

Hint for party chiefs. If we can force people to declare themselves publicly for something, we have usually also brought them to the point of declaring themselves for it privately; they want to continue to be perceived as consistent.

67

Contempt. Man is more sensitive to contempt from others than to contempt from himself.

68

Rope of gratitude. There are slavish souls who carry their thanks for favors so far that they actually strangle themselves with the rope of gratitude.

69

Trick of the prophet. In order to predict the behavior of ordinary men, we must assume that they always expend the least possible amount of intellect to free themselves from a disagreeable situation.

70

The only human right. He who strays from tradition becomes a sacrifice to the extraordinary; he who remains in tradition is its slave. Destruction follows in any case.

71

Lower than the animal. When man howls with laughter, he surpasses all animals by his coarseness.

72

Superficial knowledge. He who speaks a bit of a foreign language has more delight in it than he who speaks it well; pleasure goes along with superficial knowledge.

73

Dangerous helpfulness. There are people who want to make men's lives more difficult for no other reason than afterwards to offer them their prescriptions for making life easier – their Christianity, for example.

74

Industriousness and conscientiousness. Industriousness and conscientiousness are often antagonists, in that industriousness wants to take the fruits off the tree while still sour, but conscientiousness lets them hang too long, until they drop off the tree and come to nothing.

75

Suspicion. People whom we cannot tolerate, we try to make suspect.

76

Lacking the circumstances. Many men wait all their lives for the opportunity to be good in *their* way.

77

Want of friends. A want of friends points to envy or arrogance. Many a man owes his friends simply to the fortunate circumstance that he has no cause for envy.

78

Danger in multiplicity. With one talent the more, one often stands less secure than with one talent the less: as the table stands better on three legs than on four.

79

Model for others. He who wants to set a good example must add a grain of foolishness to his virtue; then others can imitate and, at the same time, rise above the one being imitated – something which people love.

80

Being a target. Often, other people's vicious talk about us is not actually aimed at us, but expresses their annoyance or ill humor arising from quite different reasons.

81

Easily resigned. A man suffers little from unfulfilled wishes if he has trained his imagination to think of the past as hateful.

82

In danger. When we have just gotten out of the way of a vehicle, we are most in danger of being run over.

83

The role according to the voice. He who is forced to speak more loudly than is his habit (as in front of someone hard of hearing, or before a large audience) generally exaggerates what he has to communicate.

Some people become conspirators, malicious slanderers, or schemers, merely because their voice is best suited to a whisper.

84

Love and hatred. Love and hatred are not blind, but are blinded by the fire they themselves carry with them.

85

Made an enemy to one's advantage. Men who are unable to make their merit completely clear to the world seek to awaken an intense enmity towards themselves. Then they have the comfort of thinking that this stands between their merit and its recognition – and that other people assume the same thing, which is of great advantage to their own importance.

86

Confession. We forget our guilt when we have confessed it to another, but usually the other person does not forget it.

87

Self-sufficiency. The golden fleece of self-sufficiency protects against thrashings, but not against pin-pricks.

88

Shadow in the flame. The flame is not so bright to itself as to those on whom it shines: so too the wise man.

89

Our own opinions. The first opinion that occurs to us when we are suddenly asked about a matter is usually not our own, but only the customary one, appropriate to our caste, position, or parentage; our own opinions seldom swim near the surface.

90

Origin of courage. The ordinary man is courageous and invulnerable like a hero when he does not see the danger, when he has no eyes for it. Conversely, the hero's one vulnerable spot is on his back; that is, where he has no eyes.

91

Danger in the doctor. A man is either born for his doctor, or else he perishes by his doctor.

92

Magical vanity. He who has boldly prophesied the weather three times and has been successful, believes a bit, at the bottom of his heart, in his own prophetic gift.

We do not dispute what is magical or irrational when it flatters our self-esteem.

93

Profession. A profession is the backbone of life.

94

Danger of personal influence. He who feels that he exercises a great inner influence on another must leave him quite free rein, indeed must look with favor on his occasional resistance and even bring it about: otherwise he will inevitably make himself an enemy.

95

Giving the heir his due. Whoever has established something great with a selfless frame of mind takes care to bring up heirs. It is the sign of a tyrannical and ignoble nature to see one's opponents in all the possible heirs of one's work and to live in a state of self-defense against them.

96

A little knowledge. A little knowledge is more successful than complete knowledge: it conceives things as simpler than they are, thus resulting in opinions that are more comprehensible and persuasive.

97

Not suited to be a party member. He who thinks much is not suited to be a party member: too soon, he thinks himself through and beyond the party.

98

Bad memory. The advantage of a bad memory is that, several times over, one enjoys the same good things for the first time.

99

Causing oneself pain. Inconsiderate thinking is often the sign of a discordant inner state which craves numbness.

100

Martyr. The disciple of a martyr suffers more than the martyr.

101

Residual vanity. The vanity of some people, who should not need to be vain, is the left-over and full-grown habit stemming from that time when they still had no right to believe in themselves, and only acquired their belief from others, by begging it in small change.

102

Punctum saliens of passion. He who is about to fall into a state of anger or violent love reaches a point where his soul is full like a vessel; but it needs one more drop of water: the good will to passion (which is generally also called the bad will). Only this little point is necessary; then the vessel runs over.

103

Bad-tempered thought. People are like piles of charcoal in the woods. Only when young people have stopped glowing, and carbonized, as charcoal does, do they become *useful*. As long as they smolder and smoke they are perhaps more interesting, but useless, and all too often troublesome.

Mankind unsparingly uses every individual as material to heat its great machines; but what good are the machines when all individuals (that is, mankind) serve only to keep them going? Machines that are their own end – is that the *umana commedia*?

104

The hour-hand of life. Life consists of rare, isolated moments of the greatest significance, and of innumerably many intervals, during which at best the silhouettes of those moments hover about us. Love, springtime, every beautiful melody, mountains, the moon, the sea – all these speak completely to the heart but once, if in fact they ever do get a chance to speak completely. For many men do not have those moments at all, and are themselves intervals and intermissions in the symphony of real life.

105

To set against or set to work. We often make the mistake of actively opposing a direction, or party, or epoch, because we coincidentally get to see only its superficial side, its stunted aspect, or the inescapable 'faults of its

virtues,' – perhaps because we ourselves have partici-
pated to a large degree in them. Then we turn our back
on them and seek an opposite direction; but it would be
better to look for the strong, good sides, or to develop
them in ourselves. To be sure, it takes a stronger gaze
and a better will to further that which is evolving and
imperfect, rather than to penetrate its imperfection and
reject it.

106

Modesty. True modesty (that is, the knowledge that we
are not our own creations) does exist, and it well suits
the great mind, because he particularly can comprehend
the thought of his complete lack of responsibility (even
for whatever good he creates). One does not hate the
great man's immodesty because he is feeling his strength,
but rather because he wants to feel it primarily by wound-
ing others, treating them imperiously and watching to
see how much they can stand. Most often, this actually
proves that he lacks a secure sense of his strength, and
makes men doubt his greatness. To this extent, clever-
ness would strongly advise against immodesty.

107

The first thought of the day. The best way to begin each
day well is to think upon awakening whether we could
not give at least one person pleasure on this day. If this
practice could be accepted as a substitute for the religious
habit of prayer, our fellow men would benefit by this
change.

108

Arrogance as the last means of comfort. If a man accounts for a misfortune, or his intellectual inadequacies, or his illness by seeing them as his predetermined fate, his ordeal, or mysterious punishment for something he had done earlier, he is thereby making his own nature interesting, and imagining himself superior to his fellow men. The proud sinner is a familiar figure in all religious sects.

109

Growth of happiness. Near to the sorrow of the world, and often upon its volcanic earth, man has laid out his little gardens of happiness; whether he approaches life as one who wants only knowledge from existence, or as one who yields and resigns himself, or as one who rejoices in a difficulty overcome – everywhere he will find some happiness sprouting up next to the trouble. The more volcanic the earth, the greater the happiness will be – but it would be ludicrous to say that this happiness justified suffering per se.

110

The street of one's ancestors. It is reasonable to develop further the *talent* that one's father or grandfather worked hard at, and not switch to something entirely new; otherwise one is depriving himself of the chance to attain perfection in some one craft. Thus the saying: 'Which street should you take? – that of your ancestors.'

III

Vanity and ambition as educators. So long as a man has not yet become the instrument of the universal human good, ambition may torment him; but if he has achieved that goal, if of necessity he is working like a machine for the good of all, then vanity may enter; it will humanize him in small matters, make him more sociable, tolerable, considerate, once ambition has completed the rough work (of making him useful).

112

Philosophical novices. If we have just partaken of a philosopher's wisdom, we go through the streets feeling as if we had been transformed and had become great men; for we encounter only people who do not know this wisdom, and thus we have to deliver a new, unheard-of judgment about everything; because we have acknowledged a book of laws, we also think we now have to act like judges.

113

Pleasing by displeasing. People who prefer to be noticed, and thereby displease, desire the same thing as those who do not want to be noticed, and want to please, only to a much greater degree and indirectly, by means of a step that seems to be distancing them from their goal. Because they want to have influence and power, they display their superiority, even if it is felt as disagreeable: for they know that the man who has finally gained power pleases in almost everything he does and says, that even when he displeases, he seems nevertheless to be pleasing.

Both the free spirit and the true believer want power, too, in order to use it to please; if they are threatened because of their doctrines with a dire fate, persecution, prison, or execution, they rejoice at the thought that this will enable their doctrines to be engraved and branded upon mankind; although it is delayed acting, they accept it as a painful but potent means to attain power after all.

114

Casus belli and the like. The prince who discovers a *casus belli* for an earlier decision to wage war against his neighbor is like a father who imposes a mother upon his child, to be henceforth accepted as such. And are not almost all publicly announced motives for our actions such imposed mothers?

115

Passions and rights. No one speaks more passionately about his rights than the man who, at the bottom of his heart, doubts them. In drawing passion to his side, he wants to deaden reason and its doubts: he thus gains a good conscience, and, along with it, success with his fellow men.

116

The renouncing man's trick. He who protests against marriage, in the manner of Catholic priests, will seek to understand it in its lowest, most vulgar sense. Likewise, he who refuses the respect of his contemporaries will conceive it in a base way; he thus makes his renunciation of it and the fight against it easier for himself. Incidentally, he who denies himself much in large matters will easily indulge himself in small matters. It is conceivable that the man who is above the applause of his contemporaries is nevertheless unable to refuse himself the satisfaction of little vanities.

117

The age of arrogance. The true period of arrogance for talented men comes between their twenty-sixth and thirtieth year; it is the time of first ripeness, with a good bit of sourness still remaining. On the basis of what one feels inside himself, one demands from other people, who see little or nothing of it, respect and humility; and because these are not at first forthcoming, one takes vengeance with a glance, an arrogant gesture, or a tone of voice. This a fine ear and eye will recognize in all the products of those years, be they poems, philosophies, or paintings and music. Older, experienced men smile about it, and remember with emotion this beautiful time of life, in which one is angry at his lot of having to *be* so much and *seem* so little. Later, one really *seems* to be more – but the faith in *being* much has been lost, unless one remain throughout his life vanity's hopeless fool.

118

Deceptive and yet firm. When walking around the top of an abyss, or crossing a deep stream on a plank, we need a railing, not to hold on to (for it would collapse with us at once), but rather to achieve the visual image of security.

Likewise, when we are young, we need people who unconsciously offer us the service of that railing; it is true that they would not help us if we really were in great danger and wanted to lean on them; but they give us the comforting sensation of protection nearby (for example, fathers, teachers, friends, as we generally know all three).

119

Learning to love. We must learn to love, learn to be kind, and this from earliest youth; if education or chance give us no opportunity to practice these feelings, our soul becomes dry and unsuited even to understanding the tender inventions of loving people. Likewise, hatred must be learned and nurtured, if one wishes to become a proficient hater: otherwise the germ for that, too, will gradually wither.

120

Ruins as decoration. People who go through many spiritual changes retain some views and habits from earlier stages, which then jut out into their new thinking and acting like a bit of inexplicable antiquity and gray stonework, often ornamenting the whole region.

121

Love and respect. Love desires; fear avoids. That is why it is impossible, at least in the same time span, to be loved and respected by the same person. For the man who respects another, acknowledges his power; that is, he fears it: his condition is one of awe. But love acknowledges no power, nothing that separates, differentiates, ranks higher or subordinates. Because the state of being loved carries with it no respect, ambitious men secretly or openly balk against it.

122

Prejudice in favor of cold people. People who catch fire rapidly quickly become cold, and are therefore by and large unreliable. Therefore, all those who are always cold, or act that way, benefit from the prejudice that they are especially trustworthy, reliable people: they are being confused with those others who catch fire slowly and burn for a long time.

123

What is dangerous about free opinions. The casual entertainment of free opinions is like an itch; giving in to it, one begins to rub the area; finally there is an open, aching wound; that is, the free opinion finally begins to disturb and torment us in our attitude to life, in our human relationships.

124

Desire for deep pain. When it has gone, passion leaves behind a dark longing for itself, and in disappearing throws us one last seductive glance. There must have been a kind of pleasure in having been beaten with her whip. In contrast, the more moderate feelings appear flat; apparently we still prefer a more violent displeasure to a weak pleasure.

125

Annoyance with others and the world. When, as happens so often, we let our annoyance out on others, while we are actually feeling it about ourselves, we are basically trying to cloud and delude our judgment; we want to motivate our annoyance *a posteriori* by the oversights and inadequacies of others, so we can lose sight of ourselves.

Religiously strict people, who judge themselves without mercy, are also those who have most often spoken ill of mankind in general. There has never been a saint who reserves sins to himself and virtues to others: he is as rare as the man who, following Buddha's precept, hides his goodness from people and lets them see of himself only what is bad.

126

Cause and effect confused. Unconsciously we seek out the principles and dogmas that are in keeping with our temperament, so that in the end it looks as if the principles and dogmas had created our character, given it stability and certainty, while precisely the opposite has occurred. It seems that our thinking and judging are to be made the cause of our nature after the fact, but actually our nature causes us to think and judge one way or the other.

And what decides us on this almost unconscious comedy? Laziness and convenience, and not least the vain desire to be considered consistent through and through, uniform both in character and thought: for this earns us respect, brings us trust and power.

127

Age and truth. Young people love what is interesting and odd, no matter how true or false it is. More mature minds love what is interesting and odd about truth. Fully mature intellects, finally, love truth, even when it appears plain and simple, boring to the ordinary person; for they have noticed that truth tends to reveal its highest wisdom in the guise of simplicity.

128

People as bad poets. Just as bad poets, in the second half of a line, look for a thought to fit their rhyme, so people in the second half of their lives, having become more anxious, look for the actions, attitudes, relationships that suit those of their earlier life, so that everything will harmonize outwardly. But then they no longer have any powerful thought to rule their life and determine it anew; rather, in its stead, comes the intention of finding a rhyme.

129

Boredom and play. Need forces us to do the work whose product will quiet the need; we are habituated to work by the ever-new awakening of needs. But in those intervals when our needs are quieted and seem to sleep, boredom overtakes us. What is that? It is the habit of working as such, which now asserts itself as a new, additional need; the need becomes the greater, the greater our habit of working, perhaps even the greater our suffering from our needs. To escape boredom, man works either beyond what his usual needs require, or else he invents play, that is, work that is designed to quiet no need other than that for working in general. He who is tired of play, and has no reason to work because of new needs, is sometimes overcome by the longing for a third state that relates to play as floating does to dancing, as dancing does to walking, a blissful, peaceful state of motion: it is the artist's and philosopher's vision of happiness.

130

Instruction from pictures. If we consider a series of pictures of ourselves from the time of childhood to that of manhood, we are agreeably surprised to find that the man resembles the child more than the adolescent: probably corresponding to this occurrence, then, there has been a temporary alienation from our basic character, now overcome again by the man's collected, concentrated strength. This perception agrees with the one that all those strong influences of our passions, our teachers, or political events, which pull us about in our adolescence, later seem to be reduced to a fixed measure. Certainly, they continue to live and act in us, but our basic feeling and basic thinking have the upper hand; these influences are used as sources of power, but no longer as regulators, as happens in our twenties. Thus man's thinking and feeling appear again more in accord with that of his childhood years – and this inner fact is expressed in the external one mentioned above.

131

Voice of the years. The tone adolescents use to speak, praise, blame, or invent displeases older people because it is too loud and yet at the same time muffled and unclear, like a tone in a vault, which gains resonance because of the emptiness. For most of what adolescents think has not flowed out of the fullness of their own nature, but rather harmonizes and echoes what is thought, spoken, praised, or blamed around them. But because the feelings (of inclination and disinclination) reverberate in them much more strongly than the reasons for these feelings, there arises, when they give voice to their feeling again, that muffled, ringing tone that indicates the absence or paucity of reasons. The tone of the more mature years is rigorous, sharply punctuated, moderately loud, but like everything clearly articulated, it carries very far. Finally, old age often brings a certain gentleness and indulgence to the sound and seems to sugar it: of course, in some cases it makes it sour, too.

132

Backward and anticipating people. The unpleasant personality who is full of mistrust, who reacts with envy to his competitors' and neighbors' successes, who flares up violently at divergent opinions, is showing that he belongs to an earlier stage of culture, and is thus a relic. For the way in which he interacts with people was proper and appropriate for the conditions of an age when rule by force prevailed: he is a *backward* person. A second personality, who shares profusely in others' joy, who wins friends everywhere, who is touched by everything that grows and evolves, who enjoys other people's honors and successes, and makes no claim to the privilege of alone knowing the truth, but instead is full of modest skepticism – he is an anticipator who is reaching ahead towards a higher human culture. The unpleasant personality grows out of times when the unhewn foundation of human intercourse had still to be laid; the other lives on its highest floors, as far away as possible from the wild animal that rages and howls locked up in the cellars, beneath the foundations of culture.

133

Comfort for hypochondriacs. When a great thinker is temporarily subjected to hypochondriacal self-torments, he may say to comfort himself: 'This parasite is feeding and growing from your great strength; if that strength were less, you would have less to suffer.' The statesman may speak likewise when his jealousy and vengeful feelings, in short, the mood of a *bellum omnium contra omnes*, for which he as a nation's representative must necessarily have a great gift, occasionally intrude into his personal relations and make his life difficult.

134

Alienated from the present. There are great advantages in for once removing ourselves distinctly from our time and letting ourselves be driven from its shore back into the ocean of former world views. Looking at the coast from that perspective, we survey for the first time its entire shape, and when we near it again, we have the advantage of understanding it better on the whole than do those who have never left it.

135

Sowing and reaping on personal inadequacies. People like Rousseau know how to use their weaknesses, deficiencies, or vices as if they were the fertilizer of their talent. When Rousseau laments the depravity and degeneration of society as the unpleasant consequence of culture, this is based on his personal experience, whose bitterness makes his general condemnation so sharp, and poisons the arrows he shoots. He is relieving himself first as an individual, and thinks that he is seeking a cure that will directly benefit society, but that will also indirectly, and by means of society, benefit him too.

136

A philosophical frame of mind. Generally we strive to acquire *one* emotional stance, *one* viewpoint for all life situations and events: we usually call that being of a philosophical frame of mind. But rather than making oneself uniform, we may find greater value for the enrichment of knowledge by listening to the soft voice of different life situations; each brings its own views with it. Thus we acknowledge and share the life and nature of many by not treating ourselves like rigid, invariable, single individuals.

137

In the fire of contempt. It is a new step towards independence, once a man dares to express opinions that bring disgrace on him if he entertains them; then even his friends and acquaintances begin to grow anxious. The man of talent must pass through this fire, too; afterwards he is much more his own person.

138

Sacrifice. If there is a choice, a great sacrifice will be preferred to a small one, because we compensate ourselves for a great sacrifice with self-admiration, and this is not possible with a small one.

139

Love as a device. Whoever wants really to get to *know* something new (be it a person, an event, or a book) does well to take up this new thing with all possible love, to avert his eye quickly from, even to forget, everything about it that he finds inimical, objectionable, or false. So, for example, we give the author of a book the greatest possible head start, and, as if at a race, virtually yearn with a pounding heart for him to reach his goal. By doing this, we penetrate into the heart of the new thing, into its motive center: and this is what it means to get to know it. Once we have got that far, reason then sets its limits; that overestimation, that occasional unhinging of the critical pendulum, was just a device to entice the soul of a matter out into the open.

140

To think too well or too ill of the world. Whether we think too well or too ill of things, we will always gain the advantage of reaping a greater pleasure: if our preconceived opinion is too good we are generally investing things (experiences) with more sweetness than they actually possess. If a preconceived opinion is overly negative, it leads to a pleasant disappointment: what was pleasurable in those things in and of themselves is increased through the pleasure of our surprise.

Incidentally, a morose temperament will experience the opposite in both cases.

141

Profound people. Those people whose strength lies in the profundity of their impressions (they are generally called 'profound people') are relatively controlled and decisive when anything sudden happens: for in the first moment the impression was still shallow; only later does it *become* profound. But long-foreseen, anticipated things or people excite such natures most, and make them almost incapable of maintaining presence of mind when their wait is over.

142

Traffic with one's higher self. Everyone has his good day, when he finds his higher self; and true humanity demands that we judge someone only when he is in this condition, and not in his workdays of bondage and servitude. We should, for example, assess and honor a painter according to the highest vision he was able to see and portray. But people themselves deal very differently with this, their higher self, and often act out the role of their own self, to the extent that they later keep imitating what they were in those moments. Some regard their ideal with shy humility and would like to deny it: they fear their higher self because, when it speaks, it speaks demand-ingly. In addition, it has a ghostly freedom of coming or staying away as it wishes; for that reason it is often called a gift of the gods, while actually everything else is a gift of the gods (of chance): this, however, is the man himself.

143

Solitary people. Some people are so used to solitude with themselves that they never compare themselves to others, but spin forth their monologue of a life in a calm, joyous mood, holding good conversations with themselves, even laughing. But if they are made to compare themselves with others, they tend to a brood-ing underestimation of their selves: so that they have to be forced *to learn* again from others to have a good, fair opinion of themselves. And even from this learned opinion they will always want to detract or reduce something.

Thus one must grant certain men their solitude, and not be silly enough, as often happens, to pity them for it.

144

Without melody. There are people for whom a constant inner repose and a harmonious ordering of all their capabilities is so characteristic that any goal-directed activity goes against their grain. They are like a piece of music consisting entirely of sustained harmonious chords, with no evidence of even the beginning of a structured, moving melody. At any movement from the outside, their boat at once gains a new equilibrium on the sea of harmonic euphony. Modern people are usually extremely impatient on meeting such natures, who do not *become* anything – though it may not be said that they *are* not anything. In certain moods, however, their presence evokes that rare question: why have melody at all? Why are we not satisfied when life mirrors itself peacefully in a deep lake?

The Middle Ages was richer in such natures than we are. How seldom do we now meet a person who can keep living so peacefully and cheerfully with himself even amidst the turmoil, saying to himself like Goethe: 'The best is the deep quiet in which I live and grow against the world, and harvest what they cannot take from me by fire or sword.'

145

Life and experience. If one notices how some individuals know how to treat their experiences (their insignificant everyday experiences) so that these become a plot of ground that bears fruit three times a year; while others (and how many of them!) are driven through the waves of the most exciting turns of fate, of the most varied currents of their time or nation, and yet always stay lightly on the surface, like cork: then one is finally tempted to divide mankind into a minority (minimality) of those people who know how to make much out of little and a majority of those who know how to make a little out of much; indeed, one meets those perverse wizards who, instead of creating the world out of nothing, create nothing out of the world.

146

Seriousness in play. At sunset in Genoa, I heard from a tower a long chiming of bells: it kept on and on, and over the noise of the back streets, as if insatiable for itself, it rang out into the evening sky and the sea air, so terrible and so childish at the same time, so melancholy. Then I thought of Plato's words and felt them suddenly in my heart: *all in all, nothing human is worth taking very seriously; nevertheless . . .*

147

On convictions and justice. To carry out later, in coolness and sobriety, what a man promises or decides in passion: this demand is among the heaviest burdens oppressing mankind. To have to acknowledge for all duration the consequences of anger, of raging vengeance, of enthusiastic devotion – this can incite a bitterness against these feelings all the greater because everywhere, and especially by artists, precisely these feelings are the object of idol worship. Artists cultivate the *esteem for the passions*, and have always done so; to be sure, they also glorify the frightful satisfactions of passion, in which one indulges, the outbursts of revenge that have death, mutilation, or voluntary banishment as a consequence, and the resignation of the broken heart. In any event, they keep alive curiosity about the passions; it is as if they wished to say: without passions you have experienced nothing at all.

Because we have vowed to be faithful, even, perhaps, to a purely imaginary being, a God, for instance; because we have given our heart to a prince, a party, a woman, a priestly order, an artist, or a thinker, in the state of blind madness that enveloped us in rapture and let those beings appear worthy of every honor, every sacrifice: are we then inextricably bound? Were we not deceiving ourselves then? Was it not a conditional promise, under the assumption (unstated, to be sure) that those beings to whom we dedicated ourselves really are the beings they appeared to be in our imaginations? Are we obliged to be faithful to our errors, even if we perceive that by this faithfulness we do damage to our higher self?

No – there is no law, no obligation of that kind; we *must* become traitors, act unfaithfully, forsake our ideals again and again. We do not pass from one period of life to another without causing these pains of betrayal, and without suffering from them in turn. Should we have to guard ourselves against the upsurging of our feeling in order to avoid these pains? Would not the world then become too bleak, too ghostly for us? We want rather to ask ourselves whether these pains at a change of conviction are *necessary*, or whether they do not depend on an *erroneous* opinion and estimation. Why do we admire the man who remains faithful to his conviction and despise the one who changes it? I fear the answer must be that everyone assumes such a change is caused only by motives of baser advantage or personal fear. That is, we believe fundamentally that no one changes his opinions as long as they are advantageous to him, or at least as long as they do him no harm. But if that is the case, it bears bad testimony to the *intellectual* meaning of all convictions. Let us test how convictions come into being and observe whether they are not vastly overrated: in that way it will be revealed that the *change* of convictions too is in any case measured by false standards and that until now we have tended to suffer too much from such changes.

148

Conviction is the belief that in some point of knowledge one possesses absolute truth. Such a belief presumes, then, that absolute truths exist; likewise, that the perfect methods for arriving at them have been found; finally, that every man who has convictions makes use of these perfect methods. All three assertions prove at once that the man of convictions is not the man of scientific thinking; he stands before us still in the age of theoretical innocence, a child, however grown-up he might be otherwise. But throughout thousands of years, people have lived in such childlike assumptions, and from out of them mankind's mightiest sources of power have flowed. The countless people who sacrificed themselves for their convictions thought they were doing it for absolute truth. All of them were wrong: probably no man has ever sacrificed himself for truth; at least, the dogmatic expression of his belief will have been unscientific or half-scientific. But actually one wanted to be right because one thought he *had* to be right. To let his belief be torn from him meant perhaps to put his eternal happiness in question. With a matter of this extreme importance, the 'will' was all too audibly the intellect's prompter. Every believer of every persuasion assumed he *could* not be refuted; if the counterarguments proved very strong, he could still always malign reason in general and perhaps even raise as a banner of extreme fanaticism the 'credo quia absurdum est.' It is not the struggle of opinions that has made history so violent, but rather the struggle of belief in opinions, that is, the struggle of convictions. If only all those people who thought so highly of their conviction, who sacrificed all sorts of things to it and spared neither their honor, body nor life in its service, had devoted only half of their strength to investigating by what right they clung to this or that conviction, how they had arrived at it, then how peaceable the history of mankind would appear! How much more would be known! All the cruel scenes during the persecution of every kind of heretic would have been spared us for two reasons: first, because the inquisitors would above all have inquired within themselves, and got beyond the arrogant idea that they were defending the absolute truth; and second, because the heretics themselves would not have granted such poorly established tenets as those of all the sectarians and 'orthodox' any further attention, once they had investigated them.

149

Stemming from the time when people were accustomed to believe that they possessed absolute truth is a deep *discomfort* with all skeptical and relativistic positions on any questions of knowledge; usually we prefer to surrender unconditionally to a conviction held by people of authority (fathers, friends, teachers, princes), and we have a kind of troubled conscience if we do not do so.

This inclination is understandable and its consequences do not entitle us to violent reproaches against the development of human reason. But eventually the scientific spirit in man must bring forth that virtue of *cautious restraint*, that wise moderation that is better known in the realm of practical life than in the realm of theoretical life, and that Goethe, for example, portrayed in his Antonio, as an object of animosity for all Tassos, that is, for those unscientific and also passive natures. The man of conviction has in himself a right not to understand the man of cautious thinking, the theoretical Antonio; the scientific man, on the other hand, has no right to scold him for this; he makes allowances for him and knows besides that, in certain cases, the man will cling to him as Tasso finally does to Antonio.

150

If one has not passed through various convictions, but remains caught in the net of his first belief, he is in all events, because of just this unchangeability, a representative of *backward* cultures; in accordance with this lack of education (which always presupposes educability), he is harsh, injudicious, unteachable, without gentleness, eternally suspect, a person lacking scruples, who reaches for any means to enforce his opinion because he simply cannot understand that there have to be other opinions. In this regard, he is perhaps a source of power, and even salutary in cultures grown too free and lax, but only because he powerfully incites opposition: for in that way the new culture's more delicate structure, which is forced to struggle with him, becomes strong itself.

Essentially, we are still the same people as those in the period of the Reformation – and how should it be otherwise? But we no longer allow ourselves certain means to gain victory for our opinion: this distinguishes us from that age and proves that we belong to a higher culture. These days, if a man still attacks and crushes opinions with suspicions and outbursts of rage, in the manner of men during the Reformation, he clearly betrays that he would have burnt his opponents, had he lived in other times, and that he would have taken recourse to all the means of the Inquisition, had he lived as an opponent of the Reformation. In its time, the Inquisition was reasonable, for it meant nothing other than the general martial law which had to be proclaimed over the whole domain of the church, and which, like every state of martial law, justified the use of the extremest means, namely under the assumption (which we no longer share with those people) that one *possessed* truth in the church and *had to* preserve it at any cost, with any sacrifice, for the salvation of mankind. But now we will no longer concede so easily that anyone has the truth; the rigorous methods of inquiry have spread sufficient distrust and caution, so that we experience every man who represents opinions violently in word and deed as any enemy of our present culture, or at least as a backward person. And in fact, the fervor about having the truth counts very little today in relation to that other fervor, more gentle and silent, to be sure, for seeking the truth, a search that does not tire of learning afresh and testing anew.

152

Incidentally, the methodical search for truth itself results from those times when convictions were feuding among themselves. If the individual had not cared about *his* 'truth,' that is, about his being right in the end, no method of inquiry would exist at all; but, given the eternal struggle of various individuals' claims to absolute truth, man proceeded step by step, in order to find irrefutable principles by which the justice of the claims could be tested and the argument settled. At first decisions were made according to authorities, later the ways and means with which the ostensible truth had been found were mutually criticized; in between, there was a period when the consequences of the opposing tenet were drawn and perhaps experienced as harmful and saddening; this was to result in everyone's judging that the opponent's conviction contained an error. Finally, the *thinkers' personal struggle* sharpened their methods so much that truths could really be discovered, and the aberrations of earlier methods were exposed to everyone's eye.

153

All in all, scientific methods are at least as important as any other result of inquiry; for the scientific spirit is based on the insight into methods, and were those methods to be lost, all the results of science could not prevent a renewed triumph of superstition and nonsense. Clever people may *learn* the results of science as much as they like, one still sees from their conversation, especially from their hypotheses in conversation, that they lack the scientific spirit. They do not have that instinctive mistrust of the wrong ways of thinking, a mistrust which, as a consequence of long practice, has put its roots deep into the soul of every scientific man. For them it is enough to find any one hypothesis about a matter; then they get fired up about it and think that puts an end to it. For them, to have an opinion means to get fanatical about it and cherish it in their hearts henceforth as a conviction. If a matter is unexplained, they become excited at the first notion resembling an explanation that enters their brain; this always has the worst consequences, especially in the realm of politics.

Therefore everyone should have come to know at least *one* science in its essentials; then he knows what method is, and how necessary is the most extreme circumspection This advice should be given to women particularly, who are now the hopeless victims of all hypotheses, especially those which give the impression of being witty, thrilling, invigorating, or energizing. In fact, if one looks closer, one notices that the majority of all educated people still desire convictions and nothing but convictions from a thinker, and that only a slight minority want *certainty*. The former want to be forcibly carried away, in order to thus increase their own strength; the latter few have that matter-of-fact interest that ignores personal advantage, even the above-mentioned increase of strength. Wherever the thinker behaves like a *genius*, calling himself one, and looking down like a higher being who deserves authority, he is counting on the class in the overwhelming majority. To the extent that that kind of genius keeps up the heat of convictions and awakens distrust of the cautious and modest spirit of science, he is an enemy of truth, however much he may believe he is its suitor.

154

To be sure, there is also quite another category of genius, that of justice; and I can in no way see fit to esteem that kind lower than any philosophical, political, or artistic genius. It is its way to avoid with hearty indignation everything which blinds and confuses our judgment about things; thus it is an *enemy of convictions*, for it wants to give each thing its due, be it living or dead, real or fictive – and to do so it must apprehend it clearly. Therefore it places each thing in the best light and walks all around it with an attentive eye. Finally it will even give its due to its opponent, to blind or shortsighted 'conviction' (as men call it; women call it 'faith') – for the sake of truth.

155

Out of *passions* grow opinions; *mental sloth* lets these rigidify into *convictions*.

However, if one feels he is of a *free*, restlessly lively mind, he can prevent this rigidity through constant change; and if he is on the whole a veritable thinking snowball, then he will have no opinions at all in his head, but rather only certainties and precisely measured probabilities.

But we who are of a mixed nature, sometimes aglow with fire and sometimes chilled by intellect, we want to kneel down before justice, as the only goddess whom we recognize above us. Usually *the fire* in us makes us unjust, and in the sense of that goddess, impure; never may we touch her hand in this condition; never will the grave smile of her pleasure lie upon us. We honor her as our life's veiled Isis; ashamed, we offer her our pain as a penance and a sacrifice, when the fire burns us and tries to consume us. It is the *intellect* that saves us from turning utterly to burnt-out coals; here and there it pulls us away from justice's sacrificial altar, or wraps us in an asbestos cocoon. Redeemed from the fire, we then stride on, driven by the intellect, from opinion to opinion, through the change of sides, as noble *traitors* to all things that can ever be betrayed – and yet with no feeling of guilt.

156

The wanderer. He who has come only in part to a freedom of reason cannot feel on earth otherwise than as a wanderer – though not as a traveler *towards* a final goal, for this does not exist. But he does want to observe, and keep his eyes open for everything that actually occurs in the world; therefore he must not attach his heart too firmly to any individual thing; there must be something wandering within him, which takes its joy in change and transitoriness. To be sure, such a man will have bad nights, when he is tired and finds closed the gates to the city that should offer him rest; perhaps in addition, as in the Orient, the desert reaches up to the gate; predatory animals howl now near, now far; a strong wind stirs; robbers lead off his pack-animals. Then for him the frightful night sinks over the desert like a second desert, and his heart becomes tired of wandering. If the morning sun then rises, glowing like a divinity of wrath, and the city opens up, he sees in the faces of its inhabitants perhaps more of desert, dirt, deception, uncertainty, than outside the gates – and the day is almost worse than the night. So it may happen sometimes to the wanderer; but then, as recompense, come the ecstatic mornings of other regions and days. Then nearby in the dawning light he already sees the bands of muses dancing past him in the mist of the mountains. Afterwards, he strolls quietly in the equilibrium of his forenoon soul, under trees from whose tops and leafy corners only good and bright things are thrown down to him, the gifts of all those free spirits who are at home in mountain, wood, and solitude, and who are, like him, in their sometimes merry, sometimes contemplative way, wanderers and philosophers. Born out of the mysteries of the dawn, they ponder how the day can have such a pure, transparent, transfigured and cheerful face between the hours of ten and twelve – they seek the *philosophy of the forenoon*.

I

Fine, with one another silent,
Finer, with one another laughing –
Under heaven's silky cloth
Leaning over books and moss
With friends lightly, loudly laughing
Each one showing white teeth shining.

If I did well, let us be silent,
If I did badly, let us laugh
And do it bad again by half,
More badly done, more badly laugh,
Until the grave, when down we climb.

Friends! Well! What do you say?
Amen! Until we meet again!

2

Don't excuse it! Don't forgive!
You happy, heart-free people, give
This unreasonable book of mine
Ear and heart and sheltering!
Truly, friends, my own unreason
Did not grow to earn a curse!

Friedrich Nietzsche

What *I* find, what *I* am seeking –
Was that ever in a book?
Honor one from the fools' legion!
Learn from out of this fool's book
How reason can be brought – 'to reason'!

So then, friends, what do you say?
Amen! Until we meet again.

3 The Free Spirit

O sancta simplicitas! What strange simplification and falsi-fication mankind lives in! One can never cease to marvel once one has acquired eyes for this marvel! How we have made everything around us bright and free and easy and simple! How we have known how to bestow on our senses a passport to everything superficial, on our thoughts a divine desire for wanton gambolling and false conclusions! – how we have from the very beginning understood how to retain our ignorance so as to enjoy an almost inconceivable freedom, frivolity, impetuosity, bravery, cheerfulness of life, so as to enjoy life! And only on this now firm and granite basis of ignorance has knowledge hitherto been able to rise up, the will to knowledge on the basis of a far more powerful will, the will to non-knowledge, to the uncertain, to the untrue! Not as its antithesis but – as its refinement! For even if, here as elsewhere, *language* cannot get over its coarseness and continues to speak of antitheses where there are only degrees and many subtleties of gradation; even if likewise the incarnate tartuffery of morals which is now part of our invincible 'flesh and blood' twists the words in the mouths even of us men of knowledge: here and there we grasp that fact and laugh at how it is precisely the best knowledge that wants most to hold us in this *simplified*, altogether artificial, fabricated, falsified world, how it is willy-nilly in love with error because, as a living being, it is – in love with life!

2

After so cheerful an exordium a serious word would like to be heard: it addresses itself to the most serious. Take care, philosophers and friends of knowledge, and beware of martyrdom! Of suffering 'for the sake of truth'! Even of defending has hitherto regarded him only with artistic curiosity, in the case of many a philosopher it is easy to understand the dangerous desire to see him for once in his degeneration (degenerated into 'martyr', into stage- and platform-ranter). But if one does harbour such a desire, one has to be clear *what* it is one will get to see – merely a satyr play, merely a farcical after-piece, merely a continuing proof that the long tragedy *has come to an end*: supposing that every philosophy was in its inception a long tragedy. –

3

Every superior human being will instinctively aspire after a secret citadel where he is *set free* from the crowd, the many, the majority, where, as its exception, he may forget the rule 'man' – except in the one case in which, as a man of knowledge in the great and exceptional sense, he will be impelled by an even stronger instinct to make straight for this rule. He who, when trafficking with men, does not occasionally glisten with all the shades of distress, green and grey with disgust, satiety, sympathy, gloom and loneliness, is certainly not a man of an elevated taste; but if he does not voluntarily assume this burden and displeasure, if he continually avoids it and, as aforesaid, remains hidden quietly and proudly away in his citadel, then one thing is sure: he is not made, not predestined for knowledge. For if he were, he would one day have to say to himself: 'The devil can take my good taste! the rule is more interesting than the exception – than I, the exception!' – and would go *down*, would above all 'go in'. The study of the *average* human being, protracted, serious, and with much dissembling, self-overcoming, intimacy, bad company – all company is bad company except the company of one's equals –: this constitutes a necessary part of the life story of every philosopher, perhaps the most unpleasant and malodorous part and the part most full of disappointments. If he is lucky, however, as a favourite child of knowledge ought to be, he will encounter means of facilitating and cutting short his task – I mean so-called cynics, that is to say people who recognize yourselves! It spoils all the innocence and fine neutrality of your conscience, it makes you obstinate against rebuffs and red rags, it makes you stupid, brutal and bullish if in the struggle with danger, slander, suspicion, casting out and even grosser consequences of hostility you finally even have to act as defenders of truth on earth – as if 'truth' were so innocuous and inept a person she stood in need of defending! And precisely by you, you knights of most sorrowful countenance, you idlers and cobweb-spinners of the spirit! After all, you know well enough that it cannot matter in the least whether precisely *you* are in the right, just as no philosopher hitherto has been in the right, and that a more praiseworthy veracity may lie in every little question-mark placed after your favourite words and favourite theories (and occasionally after yourselves) than in all your solemn gesticulations and smart answers before courts and accusers! Better to step aside! Flee away and conceal yourselves! And have your masks and subtlety, so that you may be misunderstood! Or feared a little! And do not forget the garden, the garden with golden trellis-work. And have about you people who are like a garden – or like music on the waters in the evening, when the day is already becoming a memory; – choose the *good* solitude, the free, wanton, easy solitude which gives you too a right to remain in some sense good! How poisonous, how cunning, how bad every protracted war makes one when it cannot be waged with open force! How *personal* a protracted fear makes one, a protracted keeping watch for enemies, for possible enemies! These outcasts of society, long persecuted and sorely hunted – also the enforced recluses, the Spinozas and Giordano Brunos – in the end always become refined vengeance-seekers and brewers of poison, even if they do so under the most spiritual masquerade and perhaps without being themselves aware of it (just dig up the foundation of Spinoza's ethics and theology!) – not to speak of the stupidity of moral indignation, which is in the philosopher an unfailing sign that he has lost his philosophical sense of humour. The martyrdom of the philosopher, his 'sacrifice for truth', brings to light what there has been in him of agitator and actor; and if one the animal, the commonness, the 'rule' in themselves and yet still possess a degree of spirituality and appetite which constrains them to speak of themselves and their kind *before witnesses* – sometimes they even wallow in books as in their own dung. Cynicism is the only form in which common souls come close to honesty; and the higher man must prick up his ears at every cynicism, whether coarse or refined, and congratulate himself whenever a buffoon without shame or a scientific satyr speaks out in his presence. There are even cases in which fascination mingles with the disgust: namely where, by a caprice of nature, such an indiscreet goat and monkey is touched with genius, as in the case of the Abbé Galiani, the profoundest, most sharp-sighted and perhaps also dirtiest man of his century – he was far more profound than Voltaire and consequently also a good deal more silent. It is more often the case that, as already indicated, a scientific head is set on a monkey's body, a refined exceptional understanding on a common soul – no rare occurrence, for instance, among physicians and moral physiologists. And whenever anyone speaks, without bitterness, rather innocuously, of man as a belly with two needs and a head with one; wherever anyone sees, seeks and *wants* to see only hunger, sexual desire, and vanity, as though these were the actual and sole motives of human actions; in brief, whenever anyone speaks 'badly' of man – but does not speak *ill* of him – the lover of knowledge should listen carefully and with diligence, and he should in general lend an ear whenever anyone speaks without indignation. For the indignant man, and whoever is continually tearing and rending himself with his teeth (or, instead of himself, the world, or God, or society) may indeed morally speaking stand higher than the laughing and self-satisfied satyr, but in every other sense he is the more commonplace, less interesting, less instructive case. And no one *lies* so much as the indignant man.

4

It is hard to be understood: especially when one thinks and lives *gangasrotogati* among men who think and live otherwise, namely *kurmagati* or at best 'as the frog goes', *mandeikagati* – I am certainly doing everything I can to be hard to understand myself! – and one ought to be heartily grateful even for the will to some subtlety in interpretation. As regards one's 'good friends', however, who are always too indolent and think that because they are one's friends they have a right to indolence: one does well to allow them from the first some room and latitude for misunderstanding – thus one can laugh at their expense; – or get rid of them altogether, these good friends and still laugh!

5

That which translates worst from one language into another is the tempo of its style, which has its origin in the character of the race, or, expressed more physiologically, in the average tempo of its 'metabolism'. There are honestly meant translations which, as involuntary vulgarizations of the original, are almost falsifications simply because it was not possible to translate also its brave and happy tempo, which leaps over and puts behind it all that is perilous in things and words. The

German is virtually incapable of *presto* in his language: thus, it may be fairly concluded, also of many of the most daring and delightful nuances of free, free-spirited thought. Just as the *buffo* and the satyr is strange to him, in his body and in his conscience, so Aristophanes and Petronius are untranslatable for him. Everything staid, sluggish, ponderously solemn, all long-winded and boring species of style have been developed in profuse multiplicity among the Germans – pardon me for the fact that even Goethe's prose is, in its blend of elegance and stiffness, no exception: it is a reflection of the 'good old days', to which it belongs, and an expression of the German taste of a time when there still was a 'German taste': it was rococo *in moribus et artibus*. Lessing constitutes an exception, thanks to his histrionic nature, which was versed in and understood much: he, who was not for nothing the translator of Bayle and liked to flee to the neighbourhood of Diderot and Voltaire and even more to that of the Roman writers of comedy – in tempo too Lessing loved freespiritedness, escape from Germany. But how could the German language, even in the prose of a Lessing, imitate the tempo of Machiavelli, who in his *Principe* lets us breathe the subtle dry air of Florence and cannot help presenting the most serious affairs in a boisterous *allegrissimo*: not perhaps without a malicious artist's sense of the contrast he is risking – thoughts protracted, difficult, hard, dangerous and the tempo of the gallop and the most wanton good humour. Who, finally, would venture a German translation of Petronius, who was, to a greater degree than any great musician has hitherto been, a master of *presto* in invention, ideas, words – what do all the swamps of the sick wicked world, even of the 'antique world', matter when one has, like him, the feet of a wind, the blast and breath, the liberating scorn of a wind that makes everything healthy by making everything *run*! And as for Aristophanes, that transfiguring, complementary spirit for whose sake one *excuses* all Greece for having existed, assuming one has grasped in all its profundity *what* there is to be excused and transfigured here – I know of nothing that has led me to reflect more on *Plato*'s concealment and sphinx nature than that happily preserved *petit fait* that under the pillow of his death-bed there was discovered no 'Bible', nothing Egyptian, Pythagorean, Platonic – but Aristophanes. How could even a Plato have endured life – a Greek life which he had denied – without an Aristophanes!

6

Few are made for independence – it is a privilege of the strong. And he who attempts it, having the completest right to it but without being *compelled* to, thereby proves that he is probably not only strong but also daring to the point of recklessness. He ventures into a labyrinth, he multiplies by a thousand the dangers which life as such already brings with it, not the smallest of which is that no one can behold how and where he goes astray, is cut off from others, and is torn to pieces limb from limb by some cave-minotaur of conscience. If such a one is destroyed, it takes place so far from the understanding of men that they neither feel it nor sympathize – and he can no longer go back! He can no longer go back even to the pity of men!

7

Our supreme insights must – and should! – sound like follies, in certain cases like crimes, when they come impermissibly to the ears of those who are not predisposed and predestined for them. The exoteric and the esoteric as philosophers formerly distinguished them, among the Indians as among the Greeks, Persians and Moslems, in short wherever one believed in an order of rank and *not* in equality and equal rights – differ one from another not so much in that the exoteric stands outside and sees, evaluates, measures, judges from the outside, not from the inside: what is more essential is that this class sees things from below – but the esoteric sees them *from above*! There are heights of the soul seen from which even tragedy ceases to be tragic; and, taking all the woe of the world together, who could venture to assert that the sight of it would *have* to seduce and compel us to pity and thus to a doubling of that woe? . . . What serves the higher type of man as food or refreshment must to a very different and inferior type be almost poison. The virtues of the common man would perhaps indicate vice and weakness in a philosopher; it may be possible that if a lofty type of man degenerated and perished, he would only thus acquire qualities on whose account it would prove necessary in the lower world into which he had sunk henceforth to venerate him as a saint. There are books which possess an opposite value for soul and health depending on whether the lower soul, the lower vitality, or the higher and more powerful avails itself of them: in the former case they are dangerous, disintegrative books, which produces dissolution, in the latter they are herald calls challenging the most courageous to *their* courage. Books for everybody are always malodorous books: the smell of petty people clings to them. Where the people eats and drinks, even where it worships, there is usually a stink. One should not go into churches if one wants to breathe *pure* air.

8

In our youthful years we respect and despise without that art of nuance which constitutes the best thing we gain from life, and, as is only fair, we have to pay dearly for having assailed men and things with Yes and No in such a fashion. Everything is so regulated that the worst of all tastes, the taste for the unconditional, is cruelly misused and made a fool of until a man learns to introduce a little art into his feelings and even to venture trying the artificial: as genuine artists of life do. The anger and reverence characteristic of youth seem to allow themselves no peace until they have falsified men and things in such a way that they can vent themselves on them – youth as such is something that falsifies and deceives. Later, when the youthful soul, tormented by disappointments, finally turns suspiciously on itself, still hot and savage even in its suspicion and pangs of conscience: how angry it is with itself now, how it impatiently rends itself, how it takes revenge for its long self-delusion, as if it had blinded itself deliberately! During this transition one punishes oneself by distrusting one's feelings; one tortures one's enthusiasm with doubts, indeed one feels that even a good conscience is a danger, as though a good conscience were a screening of oneself and a sign that one's subtler honesty had grown weary; and above all one takes sides, takes sides on principle, *against* 'youth'. – A decade later: and one grasps that all this too – was still youth!

9

Throughout the longest part of human history – it is called prehistoric times – the value or non-value of an action was derived from its consequences: the action itself came as little into consideration as did its origin, but, in much the same way as today in China a distinction or disgrace reflects back from the child onto its parents, so it was the retroactive force of success or failure which led men to think well or ill of an action. Let us call this period the *pre-moral* period of mankind: the imperative 'know thyself!' was then still unknown. Over the past ten thousand years, on the other hand, one has in a few large tracts of the earth come step by step to the point at which it is no longer the consequences but the origin of the action which determines its value: a great event, taken as a whole, a considerable refinement of vision and standard, the unconscious after-effect of the sovereignty of aristocratic values and of belief in 'origins', the sign of a period which may be called the *moral* in the narrower sense: the first attempt at self-knowledge has been made. Instead of the consequences, the origin: what an inversion of perspectives! And certainly one achieved only after protracted struggles and vacillations! To be sure, a fateful new superstition, a peculiar narrowness of interpretation therewith became dominant: men interpreted the origin of an action in the most definite sense as origin in an *intention*; men became *unanimous* in the belief that the value of an action resided in the value of the intention behind it. The intention as the whole origin and prehistory of an action: it is under the sway of this prejudice that one has morally praised, blamed, judged and philosophized on earth almost to the present day. – But ought we not today to have arrived at the necessity of once again determining upon an inversion and shift of values, thanks to another self-examination and deepening on the part of man – ought we not to stand on the threshold of a period which should be called, negatively at first, the *extra-moral*: today, when among us immoralists at least the suspicion has arisen that the decisive value of an action resides in precisely that which is *not intentional* in it, and that all that in it which is intentional, all of it that can be seen, known, 'conscious', still belongs to its surface and skin – which, like every skin, betrays something but *conceals* still more? In brief, we believe that the intention is only a sign and symptom that needs interpreting, and a sign, moreover, that signifies too many things and which thus taken by itself signifies practically nothing – that morality in the sense in which it has been understood hitherto, that is to say the morality of intentions, has been a prejudice, a precipitancy, perhaps something provisional and precursory, perhaps something of the order of astronomy and alchemy, but in any event something that must be overcome. The overcoming of morality, in a certain sense even the self-overcoming of morality: let this be the name for that protracted secret labour which has been reserved for the subtlest, most honest and also most malicious consciences as living touchstones of the soul.

10

There is nothing for it: the feelings of devotion, self-sacrifice for one's neighbour, the entire morality of self-renunciation must be taken mercilessly to task and brought to court: likewise the aesthetics of 'disinterested contemplation' through which the emasculation of art today tries, seductively enough, to give itself a good conscience. There is much too much sugar and sorcery in those feelings of 'for others', of '*not* for me', for one not to have to become doubly distrustful here and to ask: 'are they not perhaps – *seductions*?' That they *give pleasure* – to him who has them and to him who enjoys their fruits, also to the mere spectator – does not yet furnish an argument in their *favour*, but urges us rather to caution. So let us be cautious!

11

Whatever standpoint of philosophy we may adopt today: from every point of view the *erroneousness* of the world in which we believe we live is the surest and firmest thing we can get our eyes on – we find endless grounds for it which would like to lure us to suppose a deceptive principle in the 'nature of things'. But he who makes our thinking itself, that is to say 'the mind', responsible for the falsity of the world – an honourable way out taken by every conscious or unconscious *advocatus dei* – : he who takes this world, together with space, time, form, motion, to be the result of a false *conclusion*: such a one would have good cause, to say the least, to learn finally to mistrust thinking itself: would it not have played on us the biggest hoax ever? and what guarantee would there be that it would not go on doing what it has always done? In all seriousness: the innocence of thinkers has something touching and inspiring of reverence in it which permits them even today to go up to consciousness and ask it to give them *honest* answers: whether it is 'real', for example, and why it really keeps the external world so resolutely at a distance, and other questions of the sort. The belief in 'immediate certainties' is a piece of *moral* naïvety which does honour to us philosophers: but – we ought not to be '*merely* moral' men! Apart from the moral aspect, that belief is a piece of stupidity which does us little honour! In civil life an ever-ready mistrustfulness may count as a sign of 'bad character' and thus be an imprudent thing to have: here among us, beyond the civil world and its Yes and No – what is there to stop us from being imprudent and saying: the philosopher, as the creature which has hitherto always been most fooled on earth, has by now a *right* to 'bad character' – he has today the *duty* to be distrustful, to squint wickedly up out of every abyss of suspicion. – You must forgive me this humorous expression and grimace: for I have long since learned to think differently, to judge differently on the subject of deceiving and being deceived, and I keep in readiness at least a couple of jabs in the ribs for the blind rage with which philosophers resist being deceived. Why *not*? It is no more than a moral prejudice that truth is worth more than appearance; it is even the worst-proved assumption that exists. Let us concede at least this much: there would be no life at all if not on the basis of perspective evaluations and appearances; and if, with the virtuous enthusiasm and awkwardness exhibited by some philosophers, one wanted to abolish the 'apparent world' altogether, well, assuming *you* could do that – at any rate nothing would remain of your 'truth' either! Indeed, what compels us to assume there exists any essential antithesis between 'true' and 'false'? Is it not enough to suppose grades of apparentness and as it were lighter and darker shades and tones of appearance – different *valeurs*, to speak in the language of painters? Why could the world *which is of any concern to us* – not be a fiction? And he who then objects: 'but to the fiction there belongs an author?' – could he not be met with the round retort: *why*? Does this 'belongs' perhaps not also belong to the fiction? Are we not permitted to be a little ironical now about the subject as we are about the predicate and object? Ought the philosopher not to rise above the belief in grammar? All due respect to governesses: but is it not time that philosophy renounced the beliefs of governesses?

12

Oh Voltaire! Oh humanity! Oh imbecility! There is some point to 'truth', to the *search* for truth; and if a human being goes about it too humanely – *'il ne cherche le vrai que pour faire le bien'* – I wager he finds nothing!

13

Granted that nothing is 'given' as real except our world of desires and passions, that we can rise or sink to no other 'reality' than the reality of our drives – for thinking is only the relationship of these drives to one another – : is it not permitted to make the experiment and ask the question whether this which is given does not *suffice* for an understanding even of the so-called mechanical (or 'material') world? I do not mean as a deception, an 'appearance', an 'idea' (in the Berkeleyan and Schopenhaueran sense), but as possessing the same degree of reality as our emotions themselves – as a more primitive form of the world of emotions in which everything still lies locked in mighty unity and then branches out and develops in the organic process (also, as is only fair, is made weaker and more sensitive), as a kind of instinctual life in which all organic functions, together with self-regulation, assimilation, nourishment, excretion, metabolism, are still synthetically bound together – as an *antecedent form* of life? – In the end, it is not merely permitted to make this experiment: it is commanded by the conscience of *method*. Not to assume several kinds of causality so long as the experiment of getting along with one has not been taken to its ultimate limits (– to the point of nonsense, if I may say so): that is a morality of method which one may not repudiate nowadays – it follows 'from its definition', as a mathematician would say. In the end, the question is whether we really recognize will as *efficient*, whether we believe in the causality of will: if we do so – and fundamentally belief in *this* is precisely our belief in causality itself – then we *have* to make the experiment of positing causality of will hypothetically as the only one. 'Will' can of course operate only on 'will' – and not on 'matter' (not on 'nerves', for example –): enough, one must venture the hypothesis that wherever 'effects' are recognized, will is operating upon will – and that all mechanical occurrences, in so far as a force is active in them, are force of will, effects of will. – Granted finally that one succeeded in explaining our entire instinctual life as the development and ramification of *one* basic form of will – as will to power, as is *my* theory –; granted that one could trace all organic functions back to this will to power and could also find in it the solution to the problem of procreation and nourishment – they are *one* problem – one would have acquired the right to define *all* efficient force unequivocally as: *will to power*. The world seen from within, the world described and defined according to its 'intelligible character' – it would be 'will to power' and nothing else.

14

'What? Does that, to speak vulgarly, not mean: God is refuted but the devil is not –?' On the contrary! On the contrary, my friends! And who the devil compels you to speak vulgarly! –

15

As happened lately, in all the clarity of modern times, with the French Revolution, that gruesome and, closely considered, superfluous farce, into which, however,

noble and enthusiastic spectators all over Europe in-
terpeted from a distance their own indignations and
raptures so long and so passionately that *the text dis-
appeared beneath the interpretation*: so a noble posterity
could once again misunderstand the entire past and only
thus perhaps make the sight of it endurable. – Or rather:
has this not already happened? have we ourselves not
been this 'noble posterity'? And, in so far as we comprehend this, is it not at this moment – done with?

16

No one is likely to consider a doctrine true merely
because it makes happy or makes virtuous: excepting
perhaps the dear 'idealists', who rapturize over the good,
the true and the beautiful and let all kinds of colourful,
clumsy and good-natured desiderata swim about together
in their pond. Happiness and virtue are no arguments. But
even thoughtful spirits like to forget that making unhappy
and making evil are just as little counter-arguments.
Something might be true although at the same time
harmful and dangerous in the highest degree; indeed, it
could pertain to the fundamental nature of existence that
a complete knowledge of it would destroy one – so that
the strength of a spirit could be measured by how much
'truth' it could take, more clearly, to what degree it
needed it attenuated, veiled, sweetened, blunted, and
falsified. But there can be no doubt that for the discovery
of certain *parts* of truth the wicked and unhappy are in a
more favourable position and are more likely to succeed;
not to speak of the wicked who are happy – a species
about whom the moralists are silent. Perhaps severity

and cunning provide more favourable conditions for the formation of the strong, independent spirit and philosopher than does that gentle, sweet, yielding good-naturedness and art of taking things lightly which is prized in a scholar and rightly prized. Supposing in advance that the concept 'philosopher' is not limited to the philosopher who writes books – or, worse, writes books of *his* philosophy! – A final trait in the image of the free-spirited philosopher is provided by Stendhal, and in view of what German taste is I do not want to fail to emphasize it – for it goes *against* German taste. '*Pour être bon philosophe*', said this last great psychologist, '*il faut être sec, clair, sans illusion. Un banquier, qui a fait fortune, a une partie du caractère requis pour faire des découvertes en philosophie, c'est-à-dire pour voir clair dans ce qui est.*'

17

Everything profound loves the mask; the profoundest things of all hate even image and parable. Should not nothing less than the *opposite* be the proper disguise under which the shame of a god goes abroad? A questionable question: it would be strange if some mystic or other had not already ventured to meditate some such thing. There are occurrences of so delicate a description that one does well to bury them and make them unrecognizable with a piece of coarseness; there are acts of love and extravagant magnanimity after which nothing is more advisable than to take a stick and give the eyewitness a thrashing and so confuse his memory. Some know how to confuse and mistreat their own memory, so as to take revenge at least on this sole confidant – shame is inventive. It is not the worst things of which one is most ashamed: there is not only deceit behind a mask – there is so much goodness in cunning. I could believe that a man who had something fragile and valuable to conceal might roll through life thick and round as an old, green, thick-hooped wine barrel: the refinement of his shame would have it so. A man whose shame has depth encounters his destinies and delicate decisions too on paths which very few ever reach and of whose existence his intimates and neighbours may not know: his mortal danger is concealed from their eyes, as is the fact that he has regained his sureness of life. Such a hidden man, who instinctively uses speech for silence and concealment and is inexhaustible in evading communication, *wants* a mask of him to roam the heads and hearts of his friends in his stead, and he makes sure that it does so; and supposing he does not want it, he will one day come to see that a mask is there in spite of that – and that that is a good thing. Every profound spirit needs a mask: more, around every profound spirit a mask is continually growing, thanks to the constantly false, that is to say *shallow* interpretation of every word he speaks, every step he takes, every sign of life he gives.

18

One must test oneself to see whether one is destined for independence and command; and one must do so at the proper time. One should not avoid one's tests, although they are perhaps the most dangerous game one could play and are in the end tests which are taken before ourselves and before no other judge. Not to cleave to another person, though he be the one you love most – every person is a prison, also a nook and corner. Not to cleave to a fatherland, though it be the most suffering and in need of help – it is already easier to sever your heart from a victorious fatherland. Not to cleave to a feeling of pity, though it be for higher men into whose rare torment and helplessness chance allowed us to look. Not to cleave to a science, though it lures one with the most precious discoveries seemingly reserved precisely for *us*. Not to cleave to one's own detachment, to that voluptuous remoteness and strangeness of the bird which flies higher and higher so as to see more and more beneath it – the danger which threatens the flier. Not to cleave to our own virtues and become as a whole the victim of some part of us, of our 'hospitality' for example, which is the danger of dangers for rich and noble souls who expend themselves prodigally, almost indifferently, and take the virtue of liberality to the point where it becomes a vice. One must know how *to conserve oneself*: the sternest test of independence.

19

A new species of philosopher is appearing: I venture to baptize these philosophers with a name not without danger in it. As I divine them, as they let themselves be divined – for it pertains to their nature to *want* to remain a riddle in some respects – these philosophers of the future might rightly, but perhaps also wrongly, be described as *attempters*. This name itself is in the end only an attempt and, if you will, a temptation.

20

Are they new friends of 'truth', these coming philosophers? In all probability: for all philosophers have hitherto loved their truths. But certainly they will not be dogmatists. It must offend their pride, and also their taste, if their truth is supposed to be a truth for everyman, which has hitherto been the secret desire and hidden sense of all dogmatic endeavours. 'My judgement is *my* judgement: another cannot easily acquire a right to it' – such a philosopher of the future may perhaps say. One has to get rid of the bad taste of wanting to be in agreement with many. 'Good' is no longer good when your neighbour takes it into his mouth. And how could there exist a 'common good'! The expression is a self-contradiction: what can be common has ever but little value. In the end it must be as it is and has always been: great things are for the great, abysses for the profound, shudders and delicacies for the refined, and, in sum, all rare things for the rare.

21

After all this do I still need to say that they too will be free, *very* free spirits, these philosophers of the future – just as surely as they will not be merely free spirits, but something more, higher, greater and thoroughly different that does not want to be misunderstood or taken for what it is not. But in saying this I feel I have a *duty*, almost as much towards them as towards us, their heralds and precursors, us free spirits! – to blow away from all of us an ancient and stupid prejudice and misunderstanding which has all too long obscured the concept 'free spirit' like a fog. In all the countries of Europe and likewise in America there exists at present something that misuses this name, a very narrow, enclosed, chained-up species of spirits who desire practically the opposite of that which informs our aims and instincts – not to mention the fact that in regard to those *new* philosophers appearing they must certainly be closed windows and bolted doors. They belong, in short and regrettably, among the *levellers*, these falsely named 'free spirits' – eloquent and tirelessly scribbling slaves of the democratic taste and its 'modern ideas', men without solitude one and all, without their own solitude, good clumsy fellows who, while they cannot be denied courage and moral respectability, are unfree and ludicrously superficial, above all in their fundamental inclination to see in the forms of existing society the cause of practically *all* human failure and misery: which is to stand the truth happily on its head! What with all their might they would like to strive after is the universal green pasture happiness of the herd, with security, safety, comfort and an easier life for all; their two most oft-recited doctrines and ditties are 'equality of rights' and 'sympathy for all that suffers' – and suffering itself they take for something that has to be *abolished*. We, who are the opposite of this, and have opened our eyes and our conscience to the question where and how the plant 'man' has hitherto grown up most vigorously, we think that this has always happened under the opposite conditions, that the perilousness of his situation had first to become tremendous, his powers of invention and dissimulation (his 'spirit' –) had, under protracted pressure and constraint, to evolve into subtlety and daring, his will to life had to be intensified into unconditional will to power – we think that severity, force, slavery, peril in the street and in the heart, concealment, stoicism, the art of experiment and devilry of every kind, that everything evil, dreadful, tyrannical, beast of prey and serpent in man serves to enhance the species 'man' just as much as does its opposite – we do not say enough when we say even that much, and at any rate we are, in what we say and do not say on this point, at the *other* end from all modern ideology and herd desiderata: at its antipodes perhaps? Is it any wonder we 'free spirits' are not precisely the most communicative of spirits? that we do not want to betray in every respect *from what* a spirit can free itself and *to what* it is then perhaps driven? And as for the dangerous formula 'beyond good and evil' with which we at any rate guard against being taken for what we are not: we *are* something different from '*libres-penseurs*', '*liberi pensatori*', '*Freidenker*', or whatever else all these worthy advocates of 'modern ideas' like to call themselves. At home in many countries of the spirit, or at least having been guests there; having again and again eluded the agreeable musty nooks and corners into which predilection and prejudice, youth, origin, the accidents of people and books, or even weariness from wandering seemed to have consigned us; full of malice towards the lures of dependence which reside in honours, or money, or offices, or raptures of the senses; grateful even to distress and changeful illness because it has always liberated us from some rule and its 'prejudice', grateful to the god, devil, sheep and worm in us, curious to the point of vice, investigators to the point of cruelty, with rash fingers for the ungraspable, with teeth and stomach for the most indigestible, ready for every task that demands acuteness and sharp senses, ready for every venture thanks to a superfluity of 'free will', with fore- and back-souls into whose ultimate intentions no one can easily see, with fore- and back-grounds to whose end no foot may go, hidden under mantles of light, conquerors even though we look like heirs and prodigals, collectors and arrangers from morn till night, misers of our riches and our full-crammed cupboards, thrifty in learning and forgetting, inventive in schemata, sometimes proud of tables of categories, sometimes pedants, sometimes night owls of labour even in broad daylight; yes, even scarecrows when we need to be – and today we need to be: in so far, that is, as we are born, sworn, jealous friends of *solitude*, of our own deepest, most midnight, most midday solitude – such a type of man are we, we free spirits! and perhaps *you* too are something of the same type, you coming men? you *new* philosophers?

4 *From High Mountains: Epode*

Oh life's midday! Oh festival! Oh garden of summer! I wait in restless ecstasy, I stand and watch and wait – where are you, friends? It is you I await, in readiness day and night. Come now! It is time you were here!

Was it not for you the glacier today exchanged its grey for roses? The brook seeks you; and wind and clouds press higher in the blue, longingly they crowd aloft to look for you.

For you have I prepared my table in the highest height – who lives so near the stars as I, or who so near the depths of the abyss? My empire – has an empire ever reached so far? And my honey – who has tasted the sweetness of it?

– And there you *are*, friends! – But, alas, am *I* not he you came to visit? You hesitate, you stare – no, be angry, rather! Is it no longer – I? Are hand, step, face transformed? And *what* I am, to you friends – I am not?

Am I another? A stranger to myself? Sprung from myself? A wrestler who subdued himself too often? Turned his own strength against himself too often, checked and wounded by his own victory?

Did I seek where the wind bites keenest, learn to live where no one lives, in the desert where only the polar bear lives, unlearn to pray and curse, unlearn man and god, become a ghost flitting across the glaciers?

– Old friends! how pale you look, how full of love and terror! No – be gone! Be not angry! Here – *you* could not be at home: here in this far domain of ice and rocks – here you must be a huntsman, and like the Alpine goat.

A *wicked* huntsman is what I have become! – See how bent my bow! He who drew that bow, surely he was the mightiest of men – : but the arrow, alas – ah, *no* arrow is dangerous as *that* arrow is dangerous – away! be gone! For your own preservation! . . .

You turn away? – O heart, you have borne up well, your hopes stayed strong: now keep your door open to *new* friends! Let the old go! Let memories go! If once you were young, now – you are younger!

What once united us, the bond of *one* hope – who still can read the signs love once inscribed therein, now faint and faded? It is like a parchment – discoloured, scorched – from which the hand *shrinks back*.

No longer friends, but – what shall I call them? – they are the ghosts of friends which at my heart and window knock at night, which gaze on me and say: '*were* we once friends?' – oh faded word, once fragrant as the rose!

Oh longing of youth, which did not know itself! Those *I* longed for, those I deemed changed into kin of mine – that they have *aged* is what has banished them: only he who changes remains akin to me.

Oh life's midday! Oh second youth! Oh garden of summer! I wait in restless ecstasy, I stand and watch and wait – it is friends I await, in readiness day and night, *new* friends. Come now! It is time you were here!

This song is done – desire's sweet cry died on the lips: a sorcerer did it, the timely friend, the midday friend – no! ask not who he is – at midday it happened, at midday one became two . . .

Now, sure of victory together, we celebrate the feast of feasts: friend *Zarathrustra* has come, the guest of guests! Now the world is laughing, the dread curtain is rent, the wedding day has come for light and darkness . . .

THE STORY OF PENGUIN CLASSICS

Before 1946 ... 'Classics' are mainly the domain of academics and students; readable editions for everyone else are almost unheard of. This all changes when a little-known classicist, E. V. Rieu, presents Penguin founder Allen Lane with the translation of Homer's *Odyssey* that he has been working on in his spare time.

1946 Penguin Classics debuts with *The Odyssey*, which promptly sells three million copies. Suddenly, classics are no longer for the privileged few.

1950s Rieu, now series editor, turns to professional writers for the best modern, readable translations, including Dorothy L. Sayers's *Inferno* and Robert Graves's unexpurgated *Twelve Caesars*.

1960s The Classics are given the distinctive black covers that have remained a constant throughout the life of the series. Rieu retires in 1964, hailing the Penguin Classics list as 'the greatest educative force of the twentieth century.'

1970s A new generation of translators swells the Penguin Classics ranks, introducing readers of English to classics of world literature from more than twenty languages. The list grows to encompass more history, philosophy, science, religion and politics.

1980s The Penguin American Library launches with titles such as *Uncle Tom's Cabin*, and joins forces with Penguin Classics to provide the most comprehensive library of world literature available from any paperback publisher.

1990s The launch of Penguin Audiobooks brings the classics to a listening audience for the first time, and in 1999 the worldwide launch of the Penguin Classics website extends their reach to the global online community.

The 21st Century Penguin Classics are completely redesigned for the first time in nearly twenty years. This world-famous series now consists of more than 1300 titles, making the widest range of the best books ever written available to millions – and constantly redefining what makes a 'classic'.

The Odyssey continues ...

The best books ever written

PENGUIN 🐧 CLASSICS

SINCE 1946

Find out more at www.penguinclassics.com